Bike Tourist Magazine

Riding Bicycles in Hilton Head

Conrad Birmingham

L W Birmingham and Sons LLC

Contents

Preface

Bike Tourist Magazine was a published magazine to share the enjoyment of riding bicycles while on vacation. Five magazines were published, with an additional twenty cities visited, toured, and photographed for future publications. Each issue of Biking Tourist Magazine demonstrated the enjoyment of riding bicycles on vacation.

Bike Tourist Magazine is a bicycle magazine designed to give readers insight into how they can add bicycles to their vacation experience for a few hours per day or all day, regardless of their vacation destination. Bike Tourism Magazine highlights bicycling as an activity to add to your vacation so that your experience is unique, different, refreshing, and thrilling. You will have a growing supply of experiences, sharing local customs and people, increasing family ties, personalizing your Bike Tourist trip, and improving your pace and time. We want to build long-lasting relationships with our readers while challenging and encouraging them to change their ordinary, routine vacation into a healthy, convenient, hospitable, and people-friendly experience.

Now, these magazines have turned into a few mini-books and one book with all of the magazines. If anyone can take this knowledge and encourage them to enjoy the moment and slow down to enjoy their family and life, the books were worth developing.

Enjoy!

Introduction

You will not forget bicycling as a tourist. The traditional vacation that I had taken for the last twenty years was not working for me, and I bet you feel the same way. You go to the exact locations and do the same old thing. I needed to do something different. I wanted to see things from a new perspective.

You do not have to do the same old thing. I have written Bike Tourist Magazine to change your perspective on how you take a vacation. The benefits of riding a bicycle on your next vacation are numerous.

Here are a few:

Refreshing experience than the same old thing

Aerobic Exercise is healthy for you

Improved Attitude

The whole family can ride bicycles

Increased relationship with fellow riders – family, wife, or others

Personalized travel experience

The list of benefits is enormous, primarily related to your health and seeing things from a new perspective. I understand the magazine may not highlight your city or one you go on vacation. Bike Tourist Magazine tries to exemplify ways to experience riding your bicycles wherever you go or wherever you live.

Your life will be more fun enjoying the journey when you live in this moment. Riding your bicycle enables you to stop and soak at the moment. Driving by in a car, sunbathing on the beach, or shopping in the mall misses these opportunities to live in the moment. Sharing these moments with your family increases the pleasure of the vacation and the journey. Enjoy it and experience it.

Bicycling through cities increases the opportunities to find and enjoy unique experiences. More can be seen in a day when you personalize your vacation, and you use a bicycle for touring a city. Around any corner or behind any building is the one thing that will make your holiday memorable. These memorable moments will be more plentiful and more fulfilling because you have participated in these activities in a new way.

Bike Tourist Magazine is a bicycle magazine published to give your insight into adding bicycles as part of your vacation for a few hours a day or for all day wherever you travel on vacation. Bike Tourism Magazine highlights bicycling as an activity to add to your holiday, so your experience is unique, different, refreshing, and thrilling. You will have a growing supply of experiences, sharing local customs and people, increasing family ties, personalizing your trip, and improving your pace and time.

We want to build lasting relationships with our readers challenging them and encouraging them to change their regular, routine vacation into a healthy, convenient, hospitable, people-friendly experience. Your same old vacations will be new, and you will see things that you will not see on your typical vacation.

He is obsessed with proclaiming the benefits of riding bikes to tour cities. He launched Bike Tourist Magazine to enlighten others about the health benefits, the ease of bicycle riding, the use of quality family time, and the satisfaction of personalizing vacations. He envisions each magazine published to highlight one city from a bicycler's perspective and to emphasize the fulfilling experience of bicycle riding.

The benefits of riding bicycles are both emotional and physical. Where else can a person on vacation improve their life expectancy while riding bikes at their pace and their leisure? I do not want to ride my bicycle 100 miles at 20 miles per hour along a narrow road outside of a city. I want to journey to a town at my pace on my schedule, starting and stopping when the path presents a new experience, a unique insight, a new coffee shop, a new beach, a new store, a new restaurant, and the list goes on. Using a bicycle as the primary means of transportation creates an incredible number of new things to see, do, experience, and enjoy. I launched Bike Tourist Magazine to share these new things and to introduce the ease of bicycle riding while on vacation.

Bike Tourist Magazine – Hilton Head

Beaches, Bicycle Trails, Golf Courses, Restaurants Hilton Head Island, is a bicycler's paradise with so many segregated trails to ride on. You are away from cars which makes it a very safe place to ride bicycles. The island is eleven miles long, so you can go anywhere on just a bike, especially since the neighborhoods are connected through bicycle trails. Also, the sand beaches are packed hard, which makes them a smooth surface to ride bicycles on, and you can add an extra ten miles of bicycle trails to it. This is an excellent place for families and senior citizens to enjoy bicycle riding. Also, it is a good place to start riding bicycles again if you have not ridden them in a while.

Bicycling Bigger Than Golf? Why Do I Want To Ride Bicycles? Fun, Healthy, Easy, Connect To Family, Exciting Experiences, Increased Flexibility, Affordability, Exercise, Culture, Places To See, Things To Do Who Can Ride Bicycles? Adults, Families, Parents, You, Kids Grandparents, Lovers, Grandchildren, Me Children, Nieces, Nephews, And Friends Anyone. Can Participate And Ride Bicycles.

Editor Notes

Bicycle riding is becoming increasingly popular by the day. That is why more cities throughout the country are investing in the construction of additional bicycle trails for their locations. I read that bicycling is even more popular than golf now. I was an avid golfer in my youth before my knee and hip started failing. So then, I had to start doing something else for exercise and recreation. That was when I started bicycling. Bicycling is fun and healthy. I read an article describing a medical test done on up to 5,000 participants who rode their bicycles to work instead of driving there. The test results revealed that their health was so much better than those who did not ride bicycles. I do not ride my bike to work, but I do ride frequently, and I hope I am getting the exact effects that way.

Here are a few more things to do if you want a healthy lifestyle. Exercise often by riding your bicycle, walking around the block, or exercising at the gym. Watch what you eat by cutting out unhealthy sugars and carbohydrates from your diet. Then add supplements to your diets such as multivitamins, vitamin D, or vitamin B. You can find out your vitamin deficiencies through a blood test or new products like Gene Snip. Last but not least, you need to reduce your stress level, which is an open-ended question. How do I reduce my stress? Take supplements? Of course, all these things are good, but being grateful for what you have and laughing more will help reduce your stress tremendously. We take too much for granted in our lives, so be thankful for what you have and do not take things so seriously.

Conrad Birmingham Editor in Chief

Hilton Head Bike City Tourist Score

Hilton Head earned a Bike Tourist Score of 78, making it Bike Tourist Friendly.

Hilton Head has many bicycle trails segregating bicyclists from cars. This is very safe, and it makes it an excellent place for senior citizens and Friendly - Score 78 families with children to ride bicycles. Also, the beach is a bike lane too. There are miles of beaches that can be ridden upon. The beaches are marked every mile. Hilton Head is a wonderful place to visit year-round, and you can ride bicycles most of the winter. There are plenty of restaurants to try. There are many bicycle shops located throughout the island.

Overall, Hilton Head Island is a Bike Tourist-Friendly city, and it is a fun and safe place to ride bicycles.

Measurement Characteristic Score

Ease of Ride Flat surface - easy to ride

Miles of Paved Trails - 16 to 30 miles

Number of Bike Trails - Many segregated bicycle trails

Connectivity to Neighborhoods - Hilton Head is a small island, and bicycle trails connect it

Bike Culture - Many bicycles riders

Helmet Wearing- Many riders with helmets

Tourist Sites to See - Historical, People, Wildlife, Architecture, Gardens, Museums, Concerts, Scenery, Festivals, Urban views, beaches, parks

Tourist Things to Do - Resorts, Shops, Swimming, Boating, Fishing, Cooking, Cruising, Tours, Art shows, Arts

Affordable Bike Trip - Food, Bike Rentals, Hotels, Venues expense is high.

Bike Tours - No bicycle tours

Bike Rental/Bike Share - Bike Rental Shops available. No bike-share programs

Senior and Family Friendly Easy for seniors and families

Total Score 78

Who Knew this about Hilton Head

Population of 300 in 1950

Hilton Head had a population of 300 people in the early 1950s. Today, the population is 40,000 people. The island started to grow once a bridge was built to the mainland during the early 1950s. Before the bridge was built, private boats and ferries made it back and forth to the island.

Ancient Shell Rings

Hilton Head has shell rings constructed by the native Indians thousands of years ago. The Indians lived in the center of the ring, and they tossed their shells out onto piles. Shell Rings are found in many countries throughout the Americas. There is one shell ring left on Hilton Head at Sea Pines Forrest Reserve. However, two other shells ring Harbor Town Lighthouse. This lighthouse was not built for navigation. It was created to help promote Sea Pines. It is one of the most photographed things on Hilton Head Island. It is located in Harbor Town, which is somewhere you have to visit while in Hilton Head. The lighthouse was built as part of private development around Harbor Town and not as a navigational aid. Tourists can see it, and it is used for weddings and other events. This is a great place to bring the kids.

Hilton Head Bike Rentals

Bicycling is easy and safe on Hilton Head Island. There are miles of bicycle trails segregated from traffic. I did not even count the hard sand beaches where you can ride your bicycles.

Here is a list of the many bicycle rental shops:

Hilton Head Island Road Fish Bike Shop

Bike Doctor Hilton Head

Hilton Head Bike Company

Gracie's Bike Rental

Coastal Bike Rental

All American Bike

Atlantic Bicycle Rental

Seapines Bike Rental

Things to Carry

Cellphone backup charger

A cellphone charger costs $20.00, and it will recharge your cellphone. It is an excellent item to carry with you if you are going for a long bicycle ride. I take a lot of pictures, and my cellphone's battery runs down constantly. It is a sound investment.

Kindle

I do not go anywhere without my Kindle device. Kindle is Amazon's reading device, and you can download books or other media to it. I use Kindle Fire which costs approximately $50.00. It is nice to have if you want to check the news, read a book, or watch YouTube or a movie, especially if you get caught in the rain.

Duct Tape

There are thousands of uses for duct tape. I do not know what might happen to where you would need it while bicycling but let me speculate on a few possibilities. If you have long pants and they are getting stuck in the chain, you can duct tape your pant legs to stop this from happening. If you have a big hole in your tire and the inner tube is sticking through, you can use duct tape as a barrier between the inner tube and tire. If you fall and scrape your leg, it a bandage on your leg to clot the bleeding. There are plenty of uses for duct tape, and if you do not use it on bicycle trips, you will know where to find it if you cannot find your duct tape in the house.

History of Hilton Head

Hilton Head and War

Pre-Colonial Period and Colonial Period Spanish, French, Scots, English Many nationalities tried to settle in Port Royal Sound, starting with the Spanish in the 1500s. The French settled there in the mid-1500s and named it Port Royal Sound, the second oldest French-named location on the North American continent. It was not until Captain William Hilton, in the mid-1600s, had named Hilton Head Island after himself that the English colonies took hold of Port Royal Sound. The Scots settled in Port Royal Sound, but the Spanish destroyed their town in the late 1600s. It was not until the 1740s that the British defeated the Spanish invaders, securing Port Royal Sound for the British.

Revolutionary War

Hilton Head was patriotic, especially for the revolution. Its neighboring island, Daufuskie, was loyal to the British Crown. There were many raids between the islands and British warships invading and burning plantations on the island.

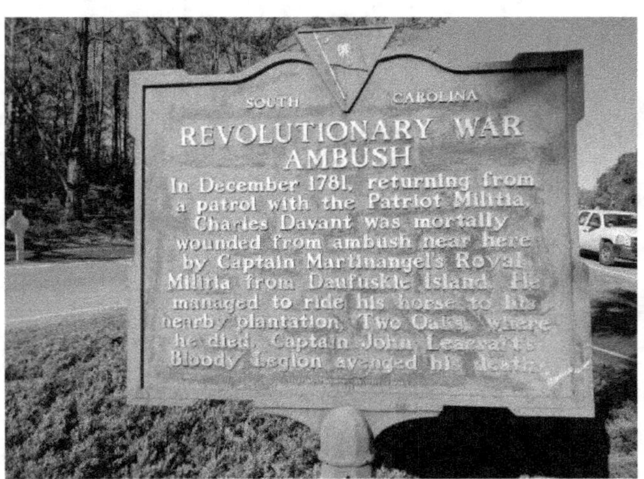

The War of 1812

The British raided and burned the plantations on the island. The island started growing cotton in the late 1700s. Civil War The Confederates occupied Hilton Head Island, securing Fort Walker. The purpose of this was to defend the entrance to Port Royal Sound. The Union attacked Port Royal Sound in the Battle of Port Royal Sound while capturing Hilton Head Island and the surrounding islands. Hilton Head became a significant Union staging area to embargo the Confederate ports. The number of Union soldiers on Hilton Head swelled to 30,000. There was a major Union hospital on the island too. During the Civil War, slaves flocked to the island so they could get their freedom. World War II Hilton Head Island had gun emplacements to defend Port Royal Sound from German raids and attacks. There were many gun emplacements along the Eastern seaboard.

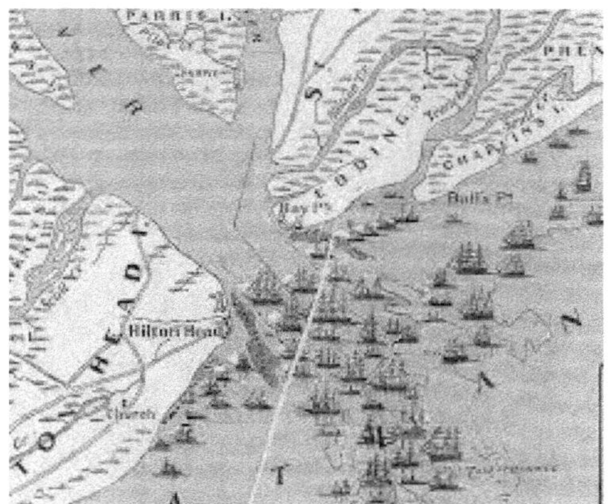

Hilton Head Development

Hilton Head was a private game reserve for the first half of the 1900s. After the bridge was built in 1956, the Sea Pine Plantation was built. Sea Pines developed Harbour Town and its distinguished lighthouse. Hilton Head Plantation was constructed soon after Sea Pines. More developments were constructed that were like Sea Pines. The population grew from 300 in the year 1955 to the 40,000 it is today. The tourists inflate the people of Hilton Head to 2.7 million annually.

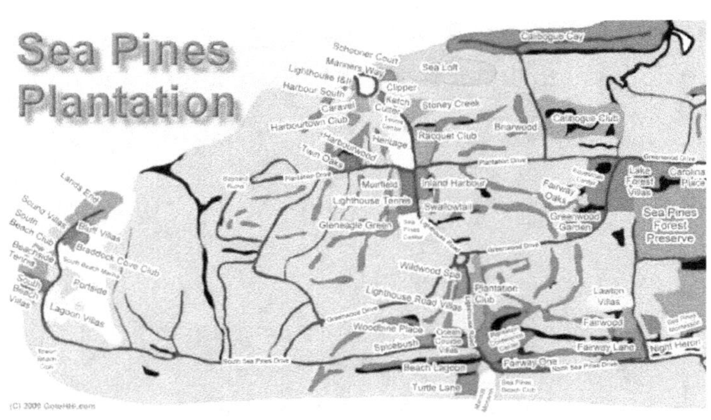

Mitchellville

Mitchelville is the Civil War and post-Civil War town which was built for escaped and emancipated slaves. Today, it is remembered as one of the first towns established for freed slaves. There is a park, beach, and earthen Civil War fort to visit. Fort Howell was built to defend the town. The beach is different than most of the other island beaches. It is rocky and not as wide. This beach faces north toward Port Royal Sound. This is an excellent beach for shells and watching birds.

Art of Biking

Healthy

Healthy Bicycle riding is beneficial because it is a form of exercise. Numerous medical studies have shown that a change in one's lifestyle, which involves more exercising, can change your health drastically for the better. The first step is to make the change and start walking or riding a bicycle. You can start in your neighborhood and walk or ride around the block to get started exercising. On weekends, you can visit a nearby park and walk or ride a bicycle. If you do not have a bike, rent one and see how you feel about riding a bike. The old saying is that you will never forget how to ride a bike once you ride a bicycle. I get some pushback from this old saying, but it is usually true. Your body might rebel because it is not used to balancing and riding a bicycle. The key is to do it but to do it consistently. Start exercising regularly, and you will see results within six months.

Food Carbohydrate Bars

It would help if you carried some energy bar or fruit bar as a snack. It is not easy to burn calories and lose energy based on many factors? Hot, windy, light breakfast, too many miles. Dropping a couple of energy bars in your backpack or bicycle saddle and eating one when you feel tired can make your bicycle ride a lot more enjoyable.

Tools

Inner Tube

Inner Tube, if you have a flat tire, it is easier to insert a new inner tube instead of patching a leak. Repairing a leak can take 30 minutes or more, while replacing an inner tube can take 10 minutes. It is quicker to use the inner tube, and it will enable you to get back riding your bicycle and enjoying your journey in a shorter amount of time. You can fix the other inner tube when you get home.

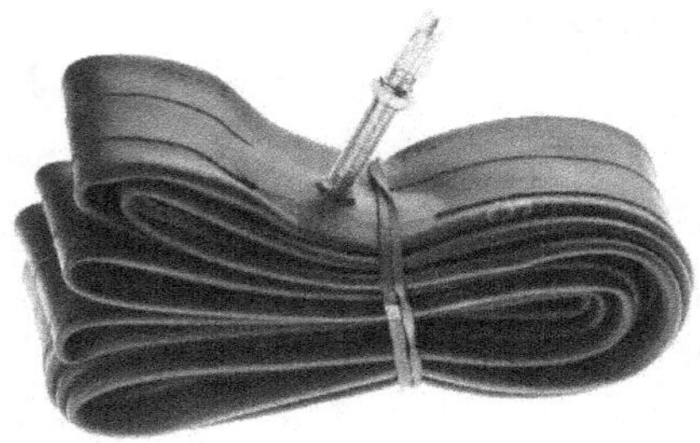

Mirror

Bicycle mirrors are necessary if you are riding with someone else. My wife and I ride bicycles, and she is following me most of the time. I am constantly turning around to see where she is, and it causes me to rock and lose my balance. If I am riding alone, it is good, but it can be a problem if someone is coming the other way or riding in a tight place. I can run into another bicycle rider or an unmovable object. There are two kinds of mirrors. One you mount to your bicycle, and the other you attach to a hat.

Cloths

Sandals

I wear tennis shoes when I ride my bicycle. Walking on beaches with tennis shoes is hard, and it feels wrong. Now, I carry my beach sandals with me when I walk on the beach because it is more comfortable. Also, it feels good to take a break from wearing my tennis shoes if I have been riding for a long time.

Exercises

Upper Thigh Stretch

Stretching is necessary every time you ride your bicycle. The most important thing to remember is that it does not help to stretch until your muscles are warm. Ride for 10 minutes, and then stretch your muscles. The Upper Thigh Stretch is excellent because you continually use your upper thigh as you pedal your bicycle. Stretch the upper thigh while you hold on to something, so you do not tip over. Take your opposite hand and bend your foot toward your back while grabbing your ankle. Slowly pull your ankle toward your back until it is tight, and hold it there for a few seconds. Repeat this exercise 5 to 10 times while pulling your ankle closer or tighter to your back if you can. This will stretch your upper thigh. Switch legs and do it on the other side.

Safety Riding Bicycles in Sand

The sand is softer than the road, and you need to be aware of the hazards of riding bicycles on surfaces that are not solid. One of the most significant hazards is turning too sharply on the sand. If you turn too sharply, your tire will act like a plow and push up the sand, stopping your bicycle dead in its tracks. I have done this, and it was not fun because I went down fast. Another hazard of riding in the sand is general fatigue. You will not ride as far and fast as you would on the road. You might be able to ride half your average distance at best.

Hilton Head Island Bike Journal

Hilton Head is a beautiful place to ride and enjoy the beach. Hilton Head Island has miles and miles of bicycle trails to ride on. We certainly enjoyed every minute of our bicycle trip to Hilton Head Island. We went to Hilton Head Island in October, and the weather was just gorgeous. It was warm but not hot. I stayed at my friend's house, and he said that most of the winter there has only mild weather conditions. This means you can bicycle throughout the entire winter season without any setbacks. My friend lives on the northern side of Hilton Head Island.

Day 1

Hilton Head

We had started the trip with a top layer of clothes to stay warm since we left earlier in the morning. But then, as the day progressed, we had to shed these clothes as the weather got warmer. We pedaled to the main bicycle trail along William Hilton Boulevard.

William Hilton Boulevard

You can move over sixty-six percent of the island by riding on William Hilton Boulevard. We went south on William Hilton Boulevard while heading toward our first stop for coffee and breakfast. Harold's Diner My friend suggested that we stop at Harold's Diner. He added that they are not the friendliest establishment, but their breakfast is fabulous. We pedaled for 30 minutes and came right up on Harold's Diner. This was a small diner in which we went in and had breakfast. The breakfast was basic but delicious. The people working there were not too interested in small talk, but their food did the talking. After breakfast, we started pedaling south on William Henry Boulevard while passing a few joggers and bicyclists. There were not too many, but there were quite a few, and you do notice them when you come to pond areas because the trail gets a little tighter in those areas.

Alligators

There were many ponds along the trail, and as we pedaled by the ponds, there were even alligators basking in the sun. It reminded me that there are alligators in every sitting body of water on the island, so I kept a closer Watch on Keeper. I would hate for my little 12-pound dog to become gator bait. Roundabout Another 30 to 40 minutes of pedaling, we came to a roundabout where William Hilton Boulevard meets Pope Avenue. In our first publication about Aruba, I talked about how hard it was to navigate a busy roundabout. In this case, the roundabout was easy to navigate because we were on the same street side that we had to turn left. We did not have to go around the circle and merge and dodge cars, making it easy. The biggest takeaway from the roundabout article is if you are scared or in doubt about negotiating a roundabout, then walk your bicycle through it as a pedestrian. We turned left from the bicycle trail to the sidewalk. We were off the bicycle trail, and we had to share the road with cars. If you do not wear a helmet, then this is when you do need one. You share the road with cars and tourists looking for things but not looking at you. Please, wear your helmet. We traveled east of Pope Avenue to Coligny Beach.

Coligny Beach

Coligny Beach Coligny Beach is an excellent public beach with many annuities. There are bicycle racks to lock your bicycles on. There are shops and restaurants too. At the beach's main entrance, there are changing rooms, restrooms, and bicycle rental shops. This is an excellent destination for enjoying the beach and many of Hilton Head Island's amenities. We were not going to the beach to layout under the sun or swim. We had too much of the island to enjoy on our bicycles, but we stopped for a coffee cup, read the news, and checked our social media. We went into the Beach House Resort, and they had a nice restaurant area with a patio right next to the Coligny Beach entrance. We had a small snack and coffee while we rested from the first leg of our bicycle ride.

After a good rest, we went north on North Forrest Beach Road. This road was not busy, and it was a peaceful ride. We rode north for a few miles, and then we turned around and went back south on South Forrest Beach Road. This road was busier, but it was not a bad ride while sharing it with cars.

Sea Pines $16.00 for Bicycles

We rode our bicycles as far as possible, switching from South Forrest Beach Road to North Sea Pines Drive. Somewhere along North Sea Pines Drive, we came to a gate that we could not enter because we were not staying on their plantation. We could pay $8.00 per person to gain access. I did not want to pay $16.00 to get access to Sea Pines. I found this a big disappointment because I thought we would ride our bicycles around Hilton Head Island. I guess that you can ride around Hilton Head Island if you pay the different plantations to enter their areas. We turned back around and traveled to Cordillio Parkway, and we rode on that street back to the roundabout at William Henry Boulevard.

It was getting close to lunch, and I had picked a spot on Broad Creek called Up the Creek Pub & Grill. We noticed a bicycle trail which took us half the way there. It was not too far from William Hilton Boulevard. We went around the roundabout by heading west on Palmetto Bay Road. We turned right on Target Road, which turns into Arrow Road. The bicycle trail followed the power lines for a few miles. It was a lovely bicycle trail, and it was peaceful traveling with no cars.

Bridge over Broad River

We had to get back on Palmetto Bay Road at the end of the trail, so we rode on a prominent shoulder. The bicycle trail ended because you must go over Broad River. The best thing about bridges is the view, and the bridge over Broad River is no different. We had a great idea of the river as well as the marsh and boats on the river. The worst thing about the bridge is that it is a good climb to get up it. I had to walk toward the top of the hill because I could not make it on my bicycle. I wonder if it was my hip replacement, knee replacement, being out of shape, or none of the above. It turned out to be none of the above. I had a bone chip in my knee which no one discovered for two years. Once it was cut out, it made my bicycle riding so much more pleasant. After we crossed the bridge, the road turned to Cross Island Parkway, and we turned right at the first road, Marshland Drive. This road had a sidewalk, and it was easy to travel down the road to Simmons Road and to Up the Creek Pub & Grill.

Up t h e Creek Pub & Grill

Up the Creek Pub & Grill is a fantastic restaurant. It has a splendid view of the marsh, the Broad River, and the bridge we had just crossed. We sat on the back porch, and they let our dog sit on the porch with us. They even brought Keeper some water which says so much about a restaurant.

Their menu had everything, and we decided to get the Grouper. This was the best meal that I could ever remember getting on the trip. I enjoyed this place for its great food and spectacular views. I would go here every time I come back. After Marshland Road, we headed back toward the place where we were staying. Marshland Road travels north, right back to William Hilton Boulevard. We were back where we started and then retired for the evening.

Day 2

Bicycling North toward Union Cemetery

The next day we bicycled to William Hilton Road and traveled west to Union Cemetery Road. The Union Cemetery was located along this road and the Union Hospital, which housed thousands of Union soldiers. These soldiers did not die from battle but disease. Over 1,500 were buried here at one time. We traveled down Union Cemetery Road while thinking there was a cemetery there. However, there was not a cemetery there anymore but just a monument to John M. Smith. He died here during the Civil War, and his friends erected the monument after the war. The soldiers who died there from the Civil War have moved to Beaufort National Cemetery long ago. At the end of Union Cemetery Road, we turned right and went north on Dillon Road. We rode on this road until we got to Beach City Road. The North side of the island was where most of the pre-Civil War and Civil War Construction occurred because of Port Royal Sound. This was the main channel to the various rivers which fed into the sound.

Mitchellville and Fort Howell On Beach City Road

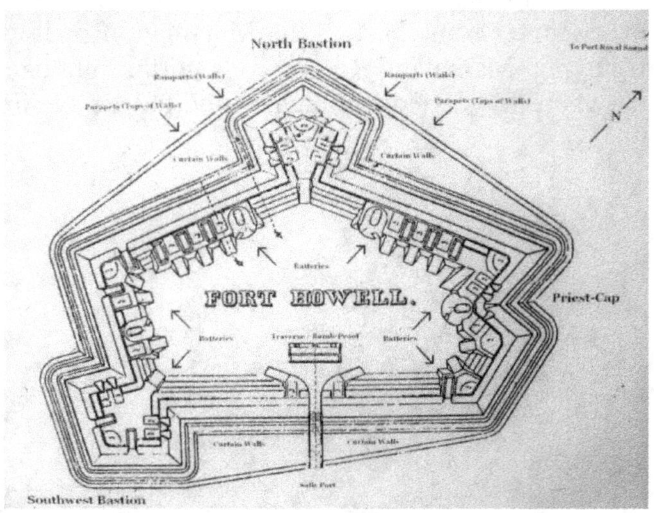

Fort Howell and Mitchellville existed during the Civil War and post-Civil War periods. Mitchellville was a town that freed slaves started. Today, there is a Preservation Center there and a park at the end of the road. A few earthworks of Fort Howell are along the road too. The Fort was built to protect Mitchellville and the northern side of the island from attack. There are no commercial businesses out here, and there is not a lot of traffic. It was an excellent place to ride bicycles without a lot of traffic or hassles.

Day 3

Beach Riding

Ride a bicycle on the beaches along the eastern coast of Hilton Head. You can ride your bike on the hard sand of the Hilton Head beaches along the east coast. What is even better is that the beach is marked with mile markers. The mile markers were placed on the beaches for emergency crews. The trip is eleven miles long, and it can take you a couple of hours to ride the distance in the sand. As a bicycle tourist, it is impossible to pass so many neat places to explore. The Number 1 marker is at South Beach, and the numbers go up to 134 Fish Haul Creek, which is on the north end of Hilton Head Island. I do not know if you can travel along the beach the whole way, but at low tide, you can. However, you can travel from mile marker 59 to 110, and you will pass many beaches and restaurants along the way.

Can you read the markers by the tenth digit so 50 to 60 is one mile and 50 to 51 is a tenth of a mile. Here are a few key markers:

59 Coligny Beach - food, drink, restrooms

61 Sea Crest - food, drinks, restrooms

71 Crown Plaza Resort

81 Disney Resort - eat, drink, restrooms

82 Marriott Beach and Golf Resort - eat, drink, restrooms

94 Coco's On the Beach - eat, drink, restrooms

98 Burke's Beach

102 Driessen Beach - Park playground

105 Folly Field Beach Park – restrooms

110 Hilton Head Beach Club - eat, drink, restrooms

If you want to be an adventurist, then travel south of marker 59 to marker 1, where you will see more sea life and the large mansions lining the beach.

When to Go - Important Dates

February - Hilton Head Island Seafood Festival

March - Hilton Head Wine and Food Fest

M ay - Hilton Head Arts Festivals

June to August - Hilton Head Harbor Fest

June to August - Hilton Head Tuesday Night Fireworks at Shelter Cove

October - Hilton Head Burgers and Brews

November - Hilton Head Island Motoring Festival

November - Hilton Head Oyster Fest

Where to Stay

Most resorts like Hilton Head Island have a selection of places to stay that are endless. There are timeshares, hotels, VBRO, beach clubs, friends, homes, condominiums, and rooms to rent. Your visit depends on how much you want to spend when you are going, and which activities you want to do. Harbor Town is an excellent place to stay because of all the activities, and you do not have to travel far to enjoy them either. Lodging near Coligny Beach is convenient to everything on the island. Anywhere on the island is convenient to everything because it is only eleven miles long. Any of the beach hotels along the eastern coast are suitable for everything as well. If you want to play golf, look for golf packages grouped in with the hotel deals. The number of places to stay at is in the thousands, close to 6,000, so you will indeed find something that meets your requirements.

What to See in Hilton Head

Beaches

Folly Field Beach Park

Folly Field Beach Park is a public beach on the island's northeastern side. This is a quiet beach. It is easy to get to, but there is limited metered parking available. Once you park, it is a short walk to a wide sandy beach area where you can walk north and south for miles. It is an excellent place to ride bicycles on the beach, though.

Driessen Beach and Burkes Beach are south of Folly Field Beach.

Coligny Beach Park

This is the best public beach on Hilton Head Island. It has a nice boardwalk with restrooms and dressing rooms. There are a few eateries and shops at the beach entrance. The beach is sandy and not rocky. It is a wide beach, and it goes north and south for miles. We rode our bicycles to this beach park on our first day's outing.

South Beach

This beach is on the island's southern tip, and it is hard to reach. At high tide, there is a tiny beach, and it has strong currents. South Beach is an excellent beach to enjoy the sunsets and to watch for dolphins. A bicycle riding along the beach is one of the best ways to get here.

Coastal Discovery

This is a great museum located on sixty acres. The museum informs you about the history of the lowlands and Hilton Head Island. It educates you about the natural habitat around the island. There are tours for the seashore, sea birds, Civil War forts, and the different habitats. Expect a good deal of walking, but it is worth every step. Tours might take 2 or 3 hours, and it is a museum you can come to time after time. You can ride your bicycle here by taking William Hilton Parkway.

Sea Pine Forrest Sea Pines Forrest Reserve

This is another excellent place to enjoy the beauty of Hilton Head Island. It is free, and it has walking trails along with guided tours. You can bicycle to Pine Forrest Reserve, but you cannot ride on the trails inside the reserve. Inside the Sea Pines, Forrest Reserve has one of the shell rings which the native Indians created thousands of years ago.

Shelter Cove Harbor

Shelter Cove Harbor is an attraction with so many things to do there. It is a marina with shops, restaurants, bicycle rentals, a golf course, fishing charters, and boat rentals. Shelter Cove Harbor is where many of the local festivals are held. This is an excellent place to stay because there are so many activities to do there.

Places to Eat

The number and quality of restaurants are limitless. As we have seen with most resort bicycling towns, there are many quality restaurants in them. There are too many to visit in just one year. These restaurants are the ones that I went to while I was riding my bicycle around Hilton Head Island.

Harold's Diner

My friend lives in Hilton Head, and he said I must go there, but remember they take cash. Also, they are northerners, and they can be rude or standoffish. This was our first stop along the bicycle path, where we had coffee and a light breakfast. The diner is located on William Hilton Boulevard, and it is a tiny diner indeed. The breakfast was great, though. If you want to make a conversation with the restaurant staff, forget it.

Tiki Hut

The Tiki Hut was our next stop at Coligny Beach. We were ready to rest and check our social media accounts and the news. We found an excellent shaded spot on their patio by the pool. We ordered coffee and a second breakfast. This restaurant is located right at the entrance to the beach, so it was very convenient. Coco's On t h e Beach Coco's was a great hamburger joint on the beach. If you are riding bicycles on the beach, look for marker # 94.

Up the Creek Pub

This was my favorite restaurant because it had a great patio looking out onto Broad Creek. The grouper here was excellent.

Skull Creek Boathouse

This is the place to go for a beautiful sunset and fabulous food. It has an outdoor seating area that was packed with people.

Adapt and Adjust

Rain, Rain!

Go to t h e Movies

 If it is going to rain the entire day or half the day, then go to the movies. But if there is just light rain for a brief time, you should still ride your bicycle. There are three great movie theaters on the island. If you do not want to go to a movie theater, there are 10 Redbox locations on the island to rent movies. That is one about every mile.

Park Plaza Cinema - middle of the island

Northridge Cinema 10 - northside of the island

Equipment Failure

If you are renting a bicycle, then call the bicycle rental shop and let them handle it. If you are riding your bike and have problems, there are up to five bicycle shops on Hilton Head Island where you can get help. This is more shops per square mile than in most locations. Two things you should do are carry a spare inner tube so that you can change out your tire quickly and perform annual maintenance on your bicycle. Let a bicycle shop look over your bike to check every spring and fix any present issues. It will reduce your stress and increase your bicycling time.

Injury

Segregated Bicycle Trails

There is less chance of an injury when you ride a segregated bicycle trail, and Hilton Head has a sizable number of segregated bicycle trails. To prevent injuries, stay on segregated bicycle trails as much as you can. Slow down and watch out at intersections and parked cars. A parked car with a door swinging open is hard to avoid. If you are injured, there are four walk-in medical clinics and one hospital on the island.

See Something Better

A day trip to Savannah is a great alternative adventure. Savannah is full of character and charm. Savannah has many neighborhoods, but the most exciting one is the downtown area with its twenty-two squares. The squares are living areas aligned with cobblestone roads. Parks are located in some of the squares. Also, downtown has a river walk along the Savannah River. This river is deep, and it allows large ships to travel up to its ports. Along the river, there are many shops and restaurants.

Did I Miss Something

Kayaking

Hilton Head Island is a fabulous place to kayak. There are plenty of places to kayak, especially the length of Broad Creek. I like the late afternoon tours, but any tour will enable you to see dolphins, birds, craps, and so much more. The landscape of the creek and marshes is peaceful. Do not miss a tranquil kayak trip. Here are a few kayaks rental shops and tours:

Kayak Hilton Head

Water Dog Outfitter s

Outside Hilton Head

Palmetto Bay Water Sport

Golfing

There are fifteen golf courses on Hilton Head Island, and there are thirty-three championship golf courses around Hilton Head. The golf courses are beautiful. Golfing is a great want to spend half a day to take a break from bicycling. Plan to play golf because it is one of the top ten destinations in the world to play golf.

Sea Pines and Harbour Town

On the south side of the island, there is Sea Pines which is a private community. It is located on 5,200 acres of land, and it houses 3,839 homes, 2,042 villas, and four championship golf courses. You can pay to gain access and visit Harbour Town with all its restaurants and shops. Also, South Beach is there too. This is an excellent place to ride bicycles because there are many things to see and do. You could plan an entire day riding in Sea Pines.

Hilton Head Plantation

On the northern side of the island, there is Hilton Head Plantation which is another private community. It is located on 4,000 acres of land and contains 4,000 homes, five hundred villas, and four golf courses. There are many activities to do in Hilton Head Plantation, such as bicycle riding, which is fun with all its bicycle trails leading through woods and marshes. If you are not staying there, then you must get a visitor's pass.

Frugal Trip

When to Travel

Traveling at the right time of the year is essential if you are on a budget and want to save money. The winter months are the least expensive because it is too cold for snowbirds. They need a consistently warmer temperature outside. Hilton Head's average temperature is 70°F during the winter holidays and then drops to the high 60s in January and the low 60s in February. If you are going to ride bicycles and explore the island, these temperatures are undoubtedly reasonable for that. Hilton Head is a little too cold to do these activities if you want to swim or lay on the beach. Just remember that you may get reasonable rental rates on houses and condominiums, but at the same time, some of the restaurants may be closed along with some of the water activities.

What's Next for Bike Tourist Magazine

Dallas

I am a huge Dallas Cowboys fan, and I have always liked the Dallas football team and the city. This next month, we highlight the city of Dallas, which has several interesting places to ride bicycles. There is a nice trail around the White Rock Lake which links up with the Deep Ellum neighborhood. Deep Ellum is an art and entertainment area that is just being developed.

A fun bicycle trail called Katy Trail Bicycle Trail is just west of downtown and heads out to Southern Methodist University (SMU). There is a high-quality restaurant there called Katy Trail Icehouse. It is a fantastic place. Near this trail is the Daily Plaza which is where John F. Kennedy was shot. It is a short bicycle ride from the Katy Trail. Dallas is a fun place to ride bicycles.

About the Author

Conrad Birmingham

Conrad Birmingham is a businessman who is retired, and he is trying to stay busy. He has no natural talent at writing any type of writing except Quality Assurance Programs, Business Plans, Bible Study Notes, Business Price Quotes, Business Memos, Loan Requests, Consulting Reports, and all things business.

He published Bike Tourist Magazine six to seven years ago, and it was a flop. After five magazines, he shut it down because it was not making money, and he became ill. Conrad visited fifteen to twenty cities, and he has experiences and pictured for these cities. Conrad hopes to include these experiences and pictures in a future book.

Conrad plans to publish seven books. One book will consolidate all five cities and the first magazine, which was an info commercial explaining what the magazine was about. This is one book out of the seven total books. The remaining five books will be individual travel guides for each city. Those books will be Aruba, Houston, South Beach, Miami, and New Orleans. All of the material is there, along with pictures, because they were published in magazines. Conrad hopes bicycle riders and vacationers find them entertaining.

Conrad has written two books of poetry over the past five years. Conrad likes four stanzas with rhyming verses. They are called Quatrains, but he does not care. They are poems with four lines that rhyme. Also, he does not like punctuation. He does not use punctuation, allowing the verses to flow as they flow. He wants the reader to figure it out, and there are no participation trophies here.

He is working on a novel and a few mini-books.